CRIME & PUNISHMENT

LAW & ORDER

Series Editor:
David Salariya was born in Dundee, Scotland, where he studied illustration and printmaking, concentrating on book design in his postgraduate year. He later completed a further postgraduate course in art education at Sussex University. He has illustrated a wide range of books on botanical, historical, and mythical subjects. He has designed and created many new series of children's books for publishers in the U.K. and overseas. In 1989 he established his own publishing company, The Salariya Book Company Ltd. He lives in Brighton, England, with his wife, the illustrator Shirley Willis.

Author:
Fiona Macdonald studied history at Cambridge University and at the University of East Anglia, where she is a part-time tutor. She has written many books for children on historical topics, including *Cities* in the *Timelines* series, and *How Would You Survive as an Aztec?*

Series Editor	David Salariya
Editor	Jenny Millington
Consultant	Jacqueline Morley
Artists	David Antram
	Mark Bergin
	Corinne Burrows
	Ray Burrows
	Simon Calder
	John James
	Syd Lewis
	Joseph McEwan
	Mark Peppé
	Gerald Wood

Artists
David Antram p 22-23, p 38-39, p 40-41; **Mark Bergin** p 42-43; **Corinne and Ray Burrows** p 8-9, p 16-17; **Simon Calder** p 30-31; **John James** p 12-13, p 14-15; **Syd Lewis** p 6-7; **Joseph McEwan** p 18-19; **Mark Peppé** p 24-25, p 26-27, p 32-33; **Gerald Wood** p 10-11, p 20-21, p 28-29, p 34-35, p 36-37.

First published in 1995
by Franklin Watts

© The Salariya Book Company Ltd MCMXCV

Printed in Belgium

Library of Congress Cataloging-in-Publication Data

Macdonald, Fiona.
  Crime and punishment / by Fiona Macdonald ; created and designed by David Salariya.
    p. cm. — (Timelines.)
  Includes index.
  Summary: Traces the history of crime and punishment from 3200 B.C. to the present and discusses how and why the laws which govern people's behavior were created.
  ISBN 0-531-14368-6 — ISBN 0-531-15280-4 (pbk.)
  1. Crime—History—Juvenile literature. 2. Criminal law—History—Juvenile literature. 3. Punishment—History—Juvenile literature. [1. Crime—History. 2. Criminal law—History. 3. Punishment—History.] I. Salariya, David. II. Title. III. Series: Timelines (Franklin Watts, Inc.)
HV6025.M29 1995
364—dc20
                                              95-10385
                                              CIP AC

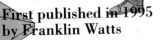

TIMELINES

CRIME & PUNISHMENT

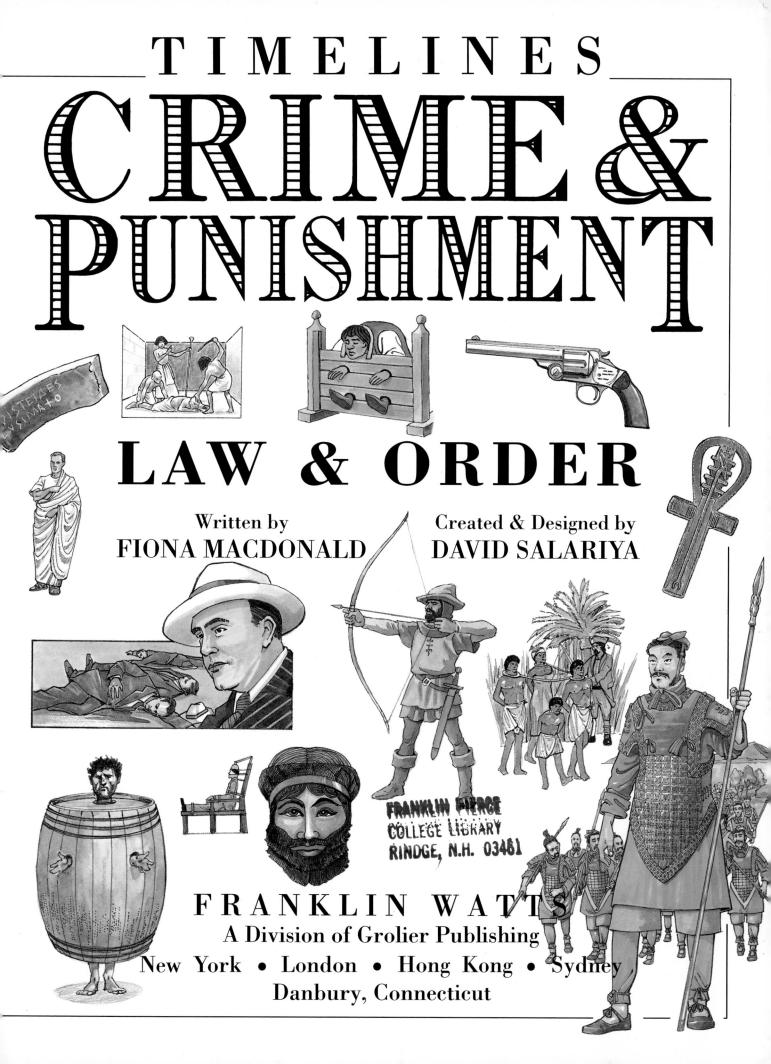

LAW & ORDER

Written by
FIONA MACDONALD

Created & Designed by
DAVID SALARIYA

FRANKLIN WATTS
A Division of Grolier Publishing
New York • London • Hong Kong • Sydney
Danbury, Connecticut

CONTENTS

THE FIRST LAWS

THE FIRST LAWS that we know about were made around 4,000 years ago by powerful kings who ruled busy, prosperous city-states in Mesopotamia (present-day Iraq). In Sumer, for example, King Ur-Nammu ordered his laws (made c. 2100 B.C.) to be carved on stone tablets and displayed in public, to deter would-be offenders. Only fragments survive, but from them we can discover what crimes and social problems Ur-Nammu hoped to control. He aimed "to protect the widow and orphan from the rich and mighty," and to regulate marriage, divorce, keeping slaves, and borrowing money.

△ HEAD from life-size statue of King Sargon of Akkad (in Babylonia). He ruled 2371 – 2230 B.C. and was a priest, lawmaker, and war leader.

△ STATUE of Gudea, governor of Lagash c. 2150 B.C.

△ GUDEA praying. He believed the gods guided him in dreams.

◁ BETWEEN 3000 B.C. and 500 B.C., many great civilizations, based in rich city states, flourished in the fertile land of Mesopotamia (present-day Iraq).

Assyria
Nineveh
Nimrud
Tigris River
Euphrates River
Babylon
Sumer
Persian Gulf

△ SUMERIAN legal contracts were written on clay tablets, then sealed in clay envelopes. This made forgery impossible.

▷ KING URU'INIMGINA ruled the city of Lagash in Sumer from 2351 to 2340 B.C. He became famous for issuing the first Sumerian "code" (collection of all known laws).

◁ KING HAMMURABI ruled in Babylon 1792-1750 B.C. His laws were carved on a stone pillar, 7 feet (2.25m) high.

◁ SUMERIAN CITIES grew rapidly under the protection of strong kings. So new laws were needed to govern market trade and to stop poor people from being exploited by the rich.

MESOPOTAMIAN NATIONS

c 3000 B.C.	Rise of city-states in Mesopotamia, ruled by strong kings.
2371 B.C.	King Sargon of Akkad establishes world's first empire.
c 2000 B.C.	Amorite peoples invade Sumer and settle in Babylon.
c 1800 B.C.	Shamshi Adad founds Assyrian kingdom.
c 1750 B.C.	Amorite King Hammurabi founds Babylonian empire.
c 840 B.C.	City-state of Urartu becomes powerful.
c 720 B.C.	Assyrians defeat Urartu, set up own empire based at Nineveh.
689 B.C.	Babylon invaded; empire collapses.
612 B.C.	Nineveh attacked; Assyrian power collapses

△ MESOPOTAMIAN KINGS passed laws to make sure that vast public works projects – like these irrigation canals in Babylon – were properly run.

▷ STRONG KINGS in Mesopotamia placed carved boundary stones at the borders of their kingdoms to show the areas that they ruled.

△ KING BAR-RAKIB of Sam'al (part of the Assyrian empire) dictates new laws to a scribe, c. A.D. 730.

◁ THE MESOPOTAMIANS used cuneiform (wedge-shaped) characters for writing. These were based on earlier picture writing: 1. Bird 2. Oasis 3. Star 4. Water. 5. Ox.

△ MESOPOTAMIAN SCRIBES scratched characters on wax-covered wooden writing boards using a reed pen.

▷ ASSYRIAN KINGS used the profits of war and justice to buy beautiful objects for their palaces, like this rhyton (ram's-horn cup) decorated with gold.

▽ ASSYRIAN SCRIBES counting heads of executed prisoners. Enemies captured in battle belonged to the king; usually he ordered them to be brutally killed.

Most criminals accused of breaking Ur-Nammu's laws were tried by unpaid judges, chosen from Sumer's leading citizens. If found guilty, they were fined. Suspects charged with serious crimes were thrown into deep water and tried by the river god. If they drowned, that showed they had been guilty. If they floated, they were innocent, and their accusers were executed instead.

In 1760 B.C., King Hammurabi of Babylon decided to collect all 282 earlier Mesopotamian laws into a single "code," covering family life, land ownership, and trade. He also introduced new, harsher punishments for many crimes. Robbers and kidnappers were executed, disobedient children became slaves, and people who caused injuries – even accidentally – were mutilated by being injured in the same way as their victims.

◁ ASSYRIANS believed that magical spirits – like this eagle-headed genie – protected them from harm, including attacks by dangerous criminals.

7

▷ AFTER DEATH, Egyptians believed that your soul was weighed against a feather. If it had been made heavy by your bad deeds, you would be punished.

EGYPT AND ISRAEL

THE MAGNIFICENT CIVILISATION of Egypt lasted from around 3200 to 332 BC. For all this time, Egypt had no written law-code. Because the Egyptians believed that their pharaohs were gods, there was no need; each pharaoh would automatically know the difference between right and wrong.

This absence of written laws did not mean that Egyptian criminals went free. Pharaohs provided justice with the help of scribes and officials, who were trained to hold courts and settle disputes over fair trade, property, wills, and inheritances.

△ PHARAOH Ramses II (1304–1237 B.C.). Pharaohs appointed a grand vizier (chief minister) to run the law courts.

△ THIS SYMBOL (called "ankh") meant life. Pharaohs were often shown holding it, because only they had the power to sentence criminals to death or to spare their lives.

CRIMES AND PUNISHMENTS

△ FARMERS often bribed royal officials to avoid paying taxes.

△ MINOR CRIMES were tried by your neighbors at local courts.

△ LONE TRAVELERS in the country might be robbed by bandits.

△ CRIMINALS were usually punished by a beating.

△ FIGHTING against the pharaoh was a crime.

◁ ON FESTIVAL DAYS, statues of the gods were carried through the streets. Victims of crimes could ask the statues to tell them who was guilty.

Court officials also had the duty to uphold legal rights for women (such as divorce) and keep detailed, written records. Junior officials acted as police, using baboons to track down criminals (like "sniffer" dogs), and arresting people who refused to pay taxes or serve in the pharaoh's army.

▷ THE GODDESS Maat received souls after death and helped judge whether the dead person's life had been good or bad.

In nearby Israel, the law was based on religious beliefs. The Jews believed that they were God's chosen people. Long ago, God had made a contract, or "covenant," with them: If they faithfully followed his laws (as taught by his prophets and recorded in the scriptures), he would guide and protect them.

These religious laws (known as the "Torah") governed all aspects of life, from what foods to eat to how to say your prayers. Religious scholars – who could interpret the Torah – became very influential. Jewish kings based their laws on religion, too. Punishments were harsh – because crime was an insult to God. They included exile, mutilation, and stoning to death.

△ THE ARK of the Covenant (a wooden casket) symbolized God's bond with the Hebrew people. At special festivals, it was carried around the temple in Jerusalem.

◁ AROUND 1200 B.C., the Hebrew prophet Moses saw Mount Sinai (in the desert between Egypt and Israel) "thundering and lightning and smoking." In the middle of all the noise, Moses heard God calling to him. He reported that God had given him carved stone tablets containing ten laws (commandments), telling the Hebrew people how to live. God had said that if the people followed these laws, they would become "a holy nation."

▽ FOR MANY CENTURIES, different races fought for the right to live in the Middle East. The strongest usually won and the Jewish people often suffered. In the seventh century B.C. the Hebrew people were taken as exiles to Babylon. They could no longer worship at their temple in Jerusalem, but they still tried, in their everyday lives, to remain faithful to the Torah (religious law).

THE TEN COMMANDMENTS

- Do not worship any other gods
- Do not make any statues or idols to worship
- Do not use God's name in vain
- Keep one day a week (the Sabbath) holy; do not work then
- Honor your father and mother
- Do not kill
- Do not commit adultery
- Do not steal
- Do not tell lies
- Do not covet (long for) your neighbor's goods

Periander, tyrant of Corinth, c. 625-585 B.C.

THE GREEKS

△ DURING the 7th century B.C., Greek city-states were ruled by "tyrants," rich businessmen who made strong laws.

△ THE TYRANTS took over from old noble families, who had ruled according to ancient traditions.

AMONG THE PEOPLES of their own time (around 700-300 B.C.) the ancient Greeks were famous for two things: their democratic system of government and their brilliant philosophers. Democracy – that is, government by the people – meant that many Greek city-states were governed by laws proposed, discussed, and voted on by ordinary citizens in public assemblies. In the city of Athens, the most famous Greek democracy, all adult male citizens could also act as jurors and try criminal cases. There were no specially trained lawyers or judges.

△ ATHENIAN CITIZENS serving in the law courts as members of a jury voted "guilty" or "not guilty" by casting ballots, into a jar.

▷ IN ATHENS, citizens met to debate new laws in the Assembly – a huge, open-air meeting.

△ BALLOTS used to cast secret votes in court.

▽ ATHENIANS voted to ostracize (exile for 10 years) leaders who had made bad decisions or had broken their laws.

△ FOR SECRECY when voting, they wrote the offenders' names on bits of pottery called "ostraka," which were collected and counted.

Punishments for criminals reflected this democratic system. A few serious offenders were condemned to death, but many more were permanently exiled or ostracized (sent away for ten years). For a Greek man, this was terrible. It meant that he lost the respect of his family, friends, and neighbors, and could no longer play a part in public life. Other convicted criminals were made to work as slaves.

▽ LIST of tribute paid to Athens by city-states in its empire. It was a crime to refuse to pay – Athens would then declare war.

△ PERICLES (c. 495-429 B.C.) ruled Athens at the peak of its power. He made the laws more democratic.

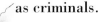

▷ WEALTHY Greek men might meet at a symposium (dinner party) to discuss city politics and ideas for new laws.

Traditionally, Greek religion taught that "the gods were just." They would reward people who lived according to the laws. But after c. 450 B.C., Greek philosophers began to ask, What did "justice" really mean? What made laws good? Should people obey all laws or only those they liked? Faced with these questions, many city-states began to treat philosophers themselves as criminals.

△ ANCIENT RELIGIOUS laws governed public behavior at religious festivals, when sacrifices were made to the gods.

◁ EVERY 4 YEARS, a special "Olympic Peace" was declared while the Olympic Games were held. Anyone who committed a crime at the games, or on their way there, was punished severely.

▷ IN ATHENS, slaves like these (working underground in the silver mines) were not trusted to give honest evidence in courts. So they were tortured first.

▷ ATHENIAN LAWS punished unfair trade and protected citizens' goods. If a politician was found guilty of a crime, all his property could be confiscated and sold.

▷ GREEK WOMEN'S lives were strictly governed by law. Unmarried girls had to obey their fathers; married women had to obey their husbands.

▽ ATHENIAN silver coin, decorated with an owl, sacred to the wise goddess Athene. She protected Athens and its laws.

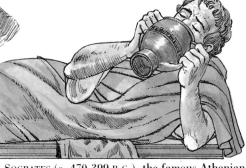

△ SOCRATES (c. 470-399 B.C.), the famous Athenian philosopher, was accused of teaching young people to criticize the government. He was found guilty but refused to apologize, so he was sentenced to death by poison. He could have escaped, but, to prove his respect for the law, he drank the poison and died.

△ IN THE CITY-STATE of Sparta, all male citizens were soldiers, ruled by a strong government and harsh laws.

Lycurgus, legendary lawmaker of Sparta, c. 600 B.C.

ROMAN CLASSES

Patricians

Plebeians

Equites

GOVERNMENT POSTS

Consul (leader of government and army).

Praetor (senior magistrate)

Quaestor (junior magistrate)

Censor (kept records of citizens and property)

Aedile (administered city's public works)

▷ IN REPUBLICAN ROME, (509-27 B.C.) society was divided into three classes: Patricians (nobles), Equites (knights), and Plebeians (workers). Government officials came mostly from the patrician class. There were many important government positions (see right).

ROME

I N 450 B.C., a committee met in Rome to produce the "Twelve Tables" – carved stone tablets that listed the laws. From then on, lawyers played a leading part in Roman life. The two consuls (government leaders) were also the chief judges, senators made new laws, and even junior officials had legal duties. As one lawyer said, it was an "honorable but exhausting" career. After A.D. 27, emperors ruled Rome. They could change the law by issuing a decree. Some emperors, like Augustus, used this power wisely to abolish outdated laws and punishments; others, like Nero, abused it by making outrageous demands. Roman criminal courts sat every day and attracted large

▽ THE ROMAN GOD Jupiter, ruler of heaven and upholder of traditional religious laws.

△ THE ROMAN SENATE was made up of past government officials. It discussed policy and voted on new laws.

▷ JULIUS CAESAR (100-44 B.C.) was a top army officer. He held many government posts but wanted still more power. He proclaimed himself "dictator for life" in 44 B.C. But soon after, he was killed by colleagues loyal to the old laws.

◁ CRIMINALS, captured enemies, and people suspected of plotting against the government were made to fight to the death as gladiators or were fed to wild beasts to entertain Roman crowds.

Julius Caesar

Gladiators

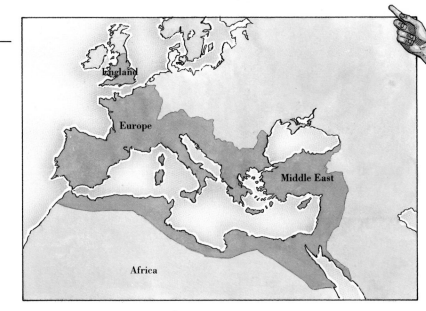

◁ THE ROMAN EMPIRE, around A.D. 100. All these lands had been conquered and were ruled by Rome. Roman governors were appointed to administer Roman law and to collect Roman taxes.

◁ MANY LOCAL TRIBES hated Roman rule, and rebelled against it. In A.D., 61 Queen Boudicca led a revolt by the people of south-east England. She and her daughters were executed.

△ REBELS and other criminals might be crucified. This was also the punishment for slaves who attacked their masters.

▷ IN A.D. 70, Jewish patriots rebelled against Roman rule. They occupied the hilltop fortress of Masada near Jerusalem. Many jumped over the cliff to their death rather than surrender.

△ AFTER Julius Caesar died, his adopted son, Octavian, seized power. In 27 B.C. the senate named him "Augustus," or emperor.

▽ THE ELITE Praetorian Guard served the emperor. Unlike other troops, they were loyal to him, rather than to the Roman senate and its laws.

crowds of spectators. Defending lawyers might hire "laudiceni" (protesters), who interrupted proceedings in court.

Punishments were graded by rank. Slaves could be beaten to death – or thrown to the lions – by their masters. Ordinary citizens could be sent to work in the silver mines. Over 6,000 rebels were crucified after an unsuccessful revolt led by the gladiator Spartacus in 71 B.C. Noble, wealthy Romans received lighter punishments; they might be exiled, be sacked from their official jobs, or have all their property taken away.

Warriors at a sacrifice, from a Celtic silver cauldron, c. A.D. 100.

△ CELTS offered human sacrifices to their god Teutates. Criminals were often chosen as victims.

CELTS, GERMANS, AND SAXONS

IN CELTIC SOCIETY, all the descendants of one great-grandfather were responsible for one another's good behavior, and the whole group might be punished for a single person's crime. Murder and insult were the most serious offenses. Druids (priests) might execute or outlaw a killer; lesser criminals might have to pay an "honor price" to compensate victims according to their rank. It was, for example, very expensive to kill a cat who guarded the king's barn. The offender had to offer a pile of grain high enough to cover the cat, held up by its tail with its nose on the floor.

△ CELTS harassed their enemies by laying a curse (*geasa*) on them. This made them commit crimes, for which they were then punished.

◁ THE MOST COMMON Celtic crimes were daring surprise raids to steal horses, chariots, and cattle.

NORTHERN EUROPE

▷ WHEN PEAT CUTTERS found this man's body in a bog in Denmark in 1950, they thought there had been a murder. In fact the body was 2,000 years old and was probably killed as a sacrifice. There was a noose around the man's neck.

△ KING CHARLEMAGNE of France (742-814) sent traveling judges throughout his kingdom.

△ BUT CHARLEMAGNE also used his power unfairly. He forced conquered tribes to become Christian.

△ CHARLEMAGNE'S new judges replaced old courts where local leaders had administered traditional law.

▽ FOR VIKINGS, pirate raids were not crimes; instead, they were a quick – if risky – way of seeking fame and fortune. Between c. 800 and 1000, Viking pirates terrorized towns and villages all around the coasts of Europe.

VIKINGS

NORTHERN EUROPEAN KINGS passed strict laws to help control their kingdoms. Royal justice was swift, and hanging was the penalty for many crimes. Otherwise, criminals had to pay victims a "wergild" (man-price), and be "pledged" to a respected community member. He would be punished if they broke the law again.

In Viking lands, crimes might be tried at the "Thing," or by juries of neighbors at local courts. There were also trials by ordeal. Men had to carry a red-hot iron bar; women had to take a stone out of boiling water. If they could not do this, or if their wounds festered, they were guilty.

△ THE LAW of the sword: insults and quarrels between Viking men might be settled by a duel.

▽ AT THE THING, the Law Speaker recited a third of the laws each year, to remind everyone how to behave.

△ LOCAL LEADERS encouraged warring families to meet to try and make peace.

△ PEOPLE who disagreed might meet to settle their quarrel by a duel.

△ OTHERWISE, criminals had to pay a heavy fine, equal in value to the damage done.

◁ MURDERERS were punished by exile. In 982, Viking exile Erik the Red left Iceland and – almost by chance – discovered Greenland.

MEDIEVAL ISLAM

LIKE THE JEWISH TORAH, the laws governing medieval Muslim lands were based on religious beliefs. Muslims respected the Jewish and Christian prophets and the Jewish and Christian scriptures in the Bible as well. But they also believed they had been sent a further – and final – message from God, telling them the right way to live. This message had been received in a series of revelations by the Prophet Muhammad, who had lived in Arabia from c. 570-632. It was written down in the book called the Koran, and it forms the basis for all Islamic law. Islamic law (called "shariyah") covered all aspects of behavior: family life, commerce, inheritance, education, worship, and war. A criminal was simply a Muslim who disobeyed God's law. The worst crime was to renounce (give up) one's faith.

▷ THESE five religious duties are often called the "Five Pillars of Islam": 1. Worship Allah (God) and no-one else. 2. Go on a pilgrimage to the House of Prayer (above) in Mecca. 3. Pray five times a day. A muezzin (speaker) calls people to prayer from the tall minaret (tower) of a mosque.

△ THE KORAN contains God's laws.

▽ LAWS made by medieval Muslim rulers said that thieves should have their right hand cut off. But in medieval Christian Europe, thieves might be hanged.

▷ 4. FAST (go without food and drink) during the holy month of Ramadan.

△ 5. GIVE MONEY to poor people and other charitable causes. This "purifies" wealth and helps society.

▷ MUSLIM SCHOLARS were world famous in the Middle Ages. Many were experts in science and mathematics; others spent their lives studying philosophy and law.

Muslim slave market

▷ THE MOST POWERFUL Muslim ruler was the caliph. He was "Commander of the Faithful" and "Defender of the Faith." All Muslim rulers were meant to govern according to Islamic law. Some did, others did not.

△ SLAVES had rights, guaranteed by law, to food, medical care, and help when they were old.

Shariyah was introduced in all the lands that came under Muslim rule. It also influenced the "dhimma" (rules) made by Muslim rulers to govern non-Muslim people living in their lands. By medieval standards, these were remarkably tolerant, though we probably would not think so today. Non-Muslims had to wear distinguishing clothing, pay special taxes, and show respect to Muslims. They could not build churches, carry swords, or live in the finest homes.

△ MUSLIM JUDGES, called *qadis*, dealt with all kinds of court cases, from forgery to family quarrels. Muslim women and children had important legal rights; women could own property, and were entitled to maintenance if their husbands deserted them.

Seige of Antioch, 1098

△ MUSLIM ARMY commanders drew up rules for "fair" war; for example, troops were not meant to harass civilians. But in siege warfare, these laws were sometimes ignored.

▽ BETWEEN the 11th and 15th centuries, Muslim and Christian armies fought wars (known as the Crusades) over possession of holy sites in the Middle East.

MEDIEVAL EUROPE

△ KING EDWARD I of England (1272-1307) with members of Parliament.

▷ COURT PROCEEDINGS were recorded in Latin on parchment by teams of expert scribes. Some court rolls might be 6.5 feet (2m) long.

△ OFFENDERS were punished by heavy fines. They were put in prison if they could not pay.

△ MINOR CRIMES like slander were punished by putting the offender in the stocks. People threw garbage at criminals trapped there, sometimes injuring them.

▽ RULERS were afraid of losing control of mobs. In towns, poor people and young apprentices rioted. In the country, poor laborers rebelled. If rebels were captured, they were accused of treason and put to death.

△ FIFTEENTH-CENTURY coins, made of real silver. Clipping coins or making forgeries were serious crimes and were sometimes dealt with very severely.

◁ GUILD MASTERS punished craftsmen who broke guild rules and regulations.

ALL MEDIEVAL EUROPEAN KINGS were responsible for giving "good justice" to their subjects. But few were as successful as, for example, Louis the Fat of France (1108-1137) or Edward I of England (1272-1307). Louis reformed royal administration and strengthened the courts. Edward worked with the "new" institution of Parliament to introduce tougher laws. Petty crimes, such as minor thefts, trespass, slander, and disputes over merchants' business or peasants' land, were still tried by local lords. But increasingly, royal justice seemed to be more trustworthy, so ordinary people began to demand the right to take their cases to the royal courts.

Even the strongest medieval kings faced problems of law and order: feuding nobles, rebellious peasants, a shortage of trained (or trustworthy) scribes and lawyers, and constant conspiracies to remove them from their thrones. Highway robbery, housebreaking, vandalism, piracy, sheep stealing, and even hooliganism were common crimes. Looting, arson, and rape always accompanied war. In peacetime, people were probably not much more violent than in Europe or the United States today, but quarrels and brawls might accidentally lead to serious injuries or even to murder, since most men carried a knife. Prison conditions were foul – no food or water was provided, so friendless prisoners might starve. Punishments were severe. Hanging was the penalty for theft, murder, arson, counterfeiting coins, and rebellion. But over half the people sent for trial for these crimes were set free.

◁ CHURCH LEADERS drew up rules for a "just war," to try and stop atrocities. But in the heat of battle, these laws were often ignored.

▷ CRIMINALS who could not be caught were declared outlaws. Rewards were offered for their capture. The English storybook hero Robin Hood may not have existed, but many outlaws did lead wild, dangerous lives in the woods.

△ ACCORDING to medieval law, a married woman's property belonged to her husband. Rich heiresses were kidnapped and married at sword point by men eager to get their wealth. Once the marriage had taken place, all the woman's land and money became theirs.

◁ LORDS IN THEIR CASTLES heard law cases and kept prisoners. They also arranged "love days" – court sessions where disputes could be settled peacefully. Some prisons had a terrible reputation. In Venice, the ruler's prison was reached by a bridge. It was called the "Bridge of Sighs," because prisoners leaving it sighed, knowing they were on their way to execution.

CHURCH LAW

△ THE POPE was head of the Roman Catholic Church. As well as providing spiritual leadership, he was also in charge of the church's own laws and law courts.

▽ WALL PAINTING, 15th-century, showing punishments awaiting sinners in hell.

MEDIEVAL EUROPEANS were subject to two different laws: state law and church law. The church had its own courts, its own lawyers, and its own legal experts (trained in church-run universities). Church law governed all kinds of behavior: marriage (and divorce), sexual behavior (homosexuality was punishable by death), private religious beliefs (it was dangerous to disagree with official church teaching), and personal morality (lying, laziness, and so on). Church courts also claimed to have powers over church members and church property all over Europe. This led to fierce arguments with many kings, who wanted absolute power over their own kingdoms.

△ CHURCH LAWS aimed to make life better for all members of society by promising rewards in heaven for good deeds done on earth and punishments in hell for crimes.

▷ A DEVIL drags a sinner down to hell.

△ DYING PEOPLE asked God's pardon for their sins to escape hell.

△ HERETICS who refused to recant were punished by being burned to death.

△ HERETICS who gave up their dissident views were whipped instead.

▽ CHURCH COURTS had their own staff of prosecutors, judges, and scribes. They had the power to try anyone – even emperors and kings. Special tribunals, called inquisitions, were set up to deal with heresy and disobedience.

△ CHURCH LAWS said it was a Christian duty to give money to charity and beggars.

△ EVERYONE was meant to confess his or her sins, and ask God's forgiveness.

△ SINNERS could show they were sorry by volunteering to be punished.

△ THEY COULD also win forgiveness by paying for church buildings and art.

Everyone had to confess his or her sins to a priest. Punishments included extra prayers, fasting (going without food), or wearing an itchy hair shirt under your clothes. People also expected to be punished in hell when they died, although you could buy expensive pardons for past sins. (Many Christians condemned this as an abuse.)

Church courts had the power of life and death. Heretics (people with "wrong" beliefs) were burned, and witches were hanged or drowned. Church lawyers argued that these harsh punishments were justified because they saved the "criminal's" soul from further sin and purified the community. After 1252, torture was permitted to force heretics and witches to confess.

▷ IN 1170, Archbishop Thomas à Becket of Canterbury was murdered on the orders of King Henry II of England, after Henry quarreled with him and with the Pope.

▷ CHURCH LAWS were debated and revised by councils of church scholars. Popes could also make new laws. Gregory X (1271-1276) was a famous lawyer and administrator.

◁ THE CHURCH censored books and learning. Sinful or heretical books might be burned. This 15th-century picture shows a "holy" book, thrown into the flames in error, miraculously leaping out of the fire.

CHINA

▷ BRONZE VESSEL, used for human or animal sacrifices, c. 1000 B.C.

△ THE GREAT WALL of China was built on the orders of Qin Shih Huang di, the first Chinese emperor (221-206 B.C.).

WHAT IS THE BEST WAY to combat crime? This question has been debated for centuries. In China, people suggested several different answers. Fortune-tellers working for Shang dynasty kings (around 1700 B.C.) relied on magic – they made sacrifices and sought advice from ancestral spirits.

The philosopher Confucius (K'ung Futzu, 551-479 B.C.) argued that laws should reward and encourage individual good behavior, rather than punish what was bad. He said that if kings were just and fair, there ought to be less crime, because everyone would want to follow the king's good example. Confucius's ideas were popular among ordinary people, but rulers hated them.

▽ DURING the Warring States period, law and order were threatened by clashes between rival armies.

△ RULERS of warring states issued their own laws and coins, like these.

◁ QIN SHIH HUANG DI also organized other vast building projects, such as roads (used by royal officials in their carriages, and by government messengers) and canals.

◁ PHILOSOPHER CONFUCIUS (551-479 B.C.) taught that laws should be made, and administered by people who showed "righteousness and humanity."

Tearing limbs   *Thousand cuts*

△ QIN SHIH HUANG DI believed in strong laws and harsh punishments. Some of his cruel tortures were used by later emperors, too.

△ QIN SHIH HUANG DI distrusted scholars and their Confucian beliefs. In 213 B.C., he ordered them and their books to be burned.

During the Warring States period, a new philosophy, called "legalism" developed. It aimed to scare people into obeying any rules and regulations, however fierce, made for the good of the state. So stern new laws and deliberately cruel punishments were introduced.

▷ STATUE of Cheng Huang, the God of Walls and Ditches. Every district had its guardian god.

◁ TO DISPLAY the power of the state and its laws, Qin Shih Huang di built a new capital city at Xianyang, near Xi'an.

JAPAN

LIKE CHINA, Japan was ruled by emperors who lived shut away from ordinary people in exquisite palace-cities. They had to rely on loyal friends and officials to maintain law and order. But in remote frontier regions, or on nobles' vast estates, the emperors' servants might be weak or lazy, and all kinds of crime might go unpunished.

Bandits robbed traveling merchants and wandering monks. Usually, they murdered their victims, because "dead men tell no tales." Along the coasts, villagers built watchtowers and fortified their homes against raids. Before the seventeenth century, Samurais' private armies brought devastation to the countryside as they waged bitter feuds.

△ ACCORDING to the Samurai code, it was more honorable to commit suicide if you were defeated in battle than to stay alive. That was shameful.

◁ TRADITIONALLY, a Japanese landowner's wealth was measured in the amount of rice that could be grown by the peasants on his estate. He had powers to make laws governing their working conditions and to regulate their wages. Some landlords were brutal. Others demanded so much rice from the peasants (as rent) that peasant families went hungry.

▽ MANY Japanese people followed the Shinto faith, which stressed absolute obedience to the emperor. Modern Shinto no longer demands this.

◁ EMMA-HOO was the Shinto god of laws and punishment, who ruled over hell and judged people when they died. He was often portrayed as a judge presiding over a law court.

▷ THE EMPEROR was the hereditary ruler of Japan, but between 1186 and 1868, shoguns issued laws in his name.

△ THE ZEN BUDDHIST FAITH was popular among samurai warriors. It taught them to be self-disciplined, rather than rely on laws made by others.

On the map: *Russian*, *Mongol*, *Ottoman*, *Mogul*

▷ THIS MAP shows the areas ruled by the different empires in Asia.

▽ INVADING Mongol armies built towers made from their enemies' skulls to warn conquered peoples not to disobey them.

ASIA

UNDER THEIR LEADER Genghis Khan (c. 1162-1227), the Mongols established the largest empire the world had ever seen, stretching from China to the Black Sea. Mongol conquests were achieved through deliberate brutality; captive enemy soldiers were used as human shields. But after the conquests, the Mongols brought peace. There was less crime in Asia than ever before. Nomad families, merchants traveling to China, and explorers like Marco Polo could all make long journeys safely overland, free from the fear of bandits, pickpockets, and cheats.

Genghis Khan

△ MONGOL LAWS divided grazing rights fairly.

△ POST-HORSE relay teams helped catch criminals.

From 1453 to 1918, the Ottoman Turks ruled an empire from their capital city of Istanbul. Ottoman laws were based on the Koran, but Ottoman sultans, like Suleyman "the Lawgiver" (1520-66), also made many new laws, trying to bring wild regions of the empire under control. Istanbul's "Palace crimes" included scandals and plots.

▽ OTTOMAN EMPERORS demanded complete obedience.

◁ LAWS were authorized by an official signature.

▷ GENERALS whose troops had been defeated faced execution as a punishment.

▷ COMMON CRIMINALS were executed by strangling.

▷ EUNUCHS kept control of all the inhabitants of the royal court.

▷ CAPTIVES and criminals might be made galley slaves.

▷ ELITE TROOPS called "janissaries" helped to maintain Ottoman law in conquered lands.

△ FEMALE CRIMINALS might be sewn into a sack and dumped at sea.

△ POLITICAL ENEMIES were assassinated by professional killers.

among the sultan's many wives, stranglings, and poisonings.

In India, Mogul emperor Akbar (1556-1605) tried to reduce economic crime by fair administration and new laws to prevent fraud. He also sought peace and justice through tolerant religious laws.

△ AKBAR introduced new laws to standardize taxes, weights, and measures.

◁ AKBAR'S foster brother, Adham Khan, was murdered for plotting against him.

△ MOGUL EMPEROR Akbar sought advice from leaders of many faiths to help him make laws that were acceptable to all his subjects.

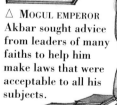

◁ EMPEROR Akbar (ruled 1556-1605) and advisors in his "house of wisdom."

◁ PUGACHEV (1742-1775) led a revolt against Russian Empress Catherine the Great. He was cruelly kept in a cage before being executed.

In Russia, Peter the Great (1672–1725) and Empress Catherine II (1762-96) preferred strict laws and cruel punishments. Peter roasted criminals alive and ordered that peasants should lose their civil rights and become the property of their lords. Catherine saw political protest as a crime and persecuted protest leaders.

◁ PETER THE GREAT of Russia (ruled 1682-1725) was over 6.5 feet (2 m) tall.

◁ PETER passed laws to ban old customs like wearing beards.

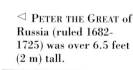

△ RUSSIAN PEASANTS were forced by law to obey (and work for) their feudal lord. But they also elected local councils to settle quarrels (left) and run village affairs.

ANCIEN REGIME

FROM THE SIXTEENTH to the eighteenth centuries, European society often seemed to be in crisis. There were mighty kings, fine writers, great scientists, and brilliant musicians. But at the same time, hundreds of thousands of people were being butchered in civil wars or in massacres, riots, burnings, and beheadings provoked by quarrels over religion. Public floggings and hangings were popular entertainments, and eager listeners enjoyed plays and ballads telling the story of the latest violent crimes. Child murder by wicked parents seemed a favorite topic.

△ LUCREZIA BORGIA (1480-1519) belonged to a powerful noble family in Italy. To harm them, she was falsely accused of poisoning.

△ IN 1642, the quarrels between King Charles I of England (above right) and Parliament turned into war. By 1646, the king had been defeated. In 1649, he was accused of treason and be-headed.

RELIGIOUS CRIMES

△ PEOPLE accused of heresy ("wrong" beliefs) were burned.

△ IN 1605, Guy Fawkes and other Catholics plotted to blow up England's Parliament.

△ SUSPECTED WITCHES were thrown in water. If they floated, they were guilty.

△ GOVERNMENTS treated tramps and vagabonds as criminals.

△ IN 1572, all 3,000 Protestants in Paris were murdered on St. Bartholemew's Day.

△ IN THE NETHERLANDS, there were fights and murders among ruling Catholics and rebel Protestants.

△ WORSHIPING as a Puritan was illegal in England. So in 1620, the Pilgrims emigrated to America.

△ DRUNKARDS were stripped, put in a barrel, and led through the streets.

Governments passed strict laws designed to stop such "crimes" – such as wandering in search of work or giving birth to an illegitimate child. All kinds of criminals made up an under-class of poor, homeless, and increasingly angry people.

◁ DURING the 17th century, lurid pamphlets, giving details of violent crimes, became popular reading.

◁ THROUGHOUT EUROPE, governments feared protests by their opponents and riots by violent mobs.

◁ GOVERNMENTS also feared protests by "sturdy beggars." If they refused to work, they could be branded (marked with a red-hot iron) or whipped.

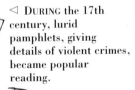

▷ ANCIEN REGIME means "the old way of ruling" - by kings rather than by representatives elected by ordinary people. Ancien Regime is used to describe governments, laws, and society in Europe between c. 1600-1789.

▽ ANCIEN REGIME punishments and executions were cruel and brutal. Most took place in public.

NATIVE AMERICANS

THERE WERE OVER two hundred Native American nations in North America. Most Native Americans agreed that the worst crimes were laziness, disloyalty, theft, and unprovoked violence. Responsible behavior was encouraged through communal ceremonies and individual rites. Young men sought a vision from a "spirit guide" – a magic bird or animal (sometimes shown as a spirit bundle) who would help them lead brave, honest lives. Punishments were based on shame and mockery or exclusion from everyday activities.

△ MANY Native American ceremonies were designed to restore harmony to the world. Dancers in the Sun Dance moved in a circle, imitating the sun in the sky.

▷ SHAMANS were magic healers, who used chanting and music to fall into a trance and enter the spirit world.

Shaman's dance hoop

Peace pipe used at council meetings

△ ADULTS disciplined children by refusing to speak to them or look at them if they behaved badly.

◁ SHAMANS' mysterious skills and sometimes frightening behavior gave them power to influence community actions, for good and evil.

△ SPIRIT BUNDLE made by a young man.

Council meeting

△ SUCCESSFUL WARRIORS became chiefs, helping to lead their nation.

Lands taken over by European Americans by 1900

Leading men met in councils to discuss how to deal with members of their nation who were behaving in a way that harmed everyone else – stealing, or refusing to work. If the offender refused to reform, they might be outlawed. This meant almost certain death; without family and friends to support them, it was hard to survive.

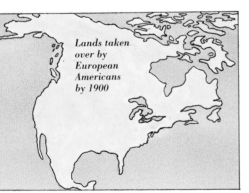

◁ NATIVE AMERICANS attacked European settlers because they took away their land.

△ NATIVE AMERICAN WARRIOR Goyathlay (Geronimo) who led the Apache Native nation against U.S. government troops. Native American leaders who fought to defend their lands were hunted and killed.

WILD WEST

URING THE 19TH CENTURY, thousands of European migrants – farmers, cattle ranchers, and miners – settled in Native American territory. During the "wars for the West" that followed, Native Americans who fought to defend their homelands were hunted and shot as criminals. There were atrocities on both sides. U.S. Army General Philip Sheridan claimed that "the only good Indian is a dead Indian," while Native American warriors stole livestock, attacked wagon trains, and kidnapped farmers' families.

△ SETTLERS living in isolated farmsteads feared attacks from Native Americans, or from gangs of vandals and robbers.

△ NATIVE AMERICANS flee for their lives as the U.S. Army attacks.

Some European settlers were honest and hard-working. But others saw the West as a land where you could "get rich quick" without having to worry too much about law and order.

◁ LAWLESS young cowboys, called hoodlums, terrorized peaceful villages and towns by racing wildly through the streets on horseback, yelling and firing guns.

▽ GUN LAW: Gunfights between drunken, off-duty cowboys or rival gold prospectors were common in Wild West towns. Men fought over girls, gambling, horses, and money.

△ THE PENALTY for killing was hanging – if the "lawmen" could catch you.

◁ CATTLE were branded with their owner's mark to stop them from being stolen by rustlers. Thieves tried to cover up the brand with their own mark.

Distances were vast. Until the transcontinental railroad was built in 1869, a runaway criminal could easily escape from the sheriff and live as an outlaw, hiding in the wild countryside. During the 1848-49 gold rush, rival miners killed one another in their fever to find gold.

▽ GANGS OF BANDITS – one of the most famous was led by outlaw Jesse James – held up stage-coaches, raided banks, and ambushed trains. James was shot dead in 1882.

◁ WILD BILL HICKOK (1837-1876). Stage-coach driver, showman and, for a time, sheriff of two frontier towns – but dismissed because he took bribes. He was a brilliant shot, once hitting (and killing) a man about 230 feet (70 m) away.

North
America

North
Atlantic
Ocean

Africa

Pacific
Ocean

South
America

South
Atlantic
Ocean

▷ PRISONERS of the
Aztec empire (c. 1300
–1521), captured in
war, were executed as
sacrifices to the gods.
They might be tied to a
stone and would then
be made to fight until
they died, armed only
with wooden weapons.

△ AZTEC JUDGES
punished crimes such
as theft and
drunkenness by death.

COLONIAL POWERS

THE FIRST European colonies
were established by Spain in
South America and the
Caribbean after 1520. The Aztecs of
Mexico and the Incas of Peru already
had strong laws, which frightened
people into good behavior.

Colonial rulers replaced these laws
with an equally harsh system of their
own. Slaves were beaten for laziness or
disobedience and could be branded
with a red-hot iron if they ran away.
Many Europeans thought slavery was a
crime, but it was not
abolished in British
colonies until 1838.

▷ IN AFRICA, war
captives and
convicted criminals
might be sold
to slave traders.

▽ ON BOARD slave
ships, the slaves were
so badly treated that
many died. Anti-
slavery campaigners
said this was murder.

▽ IN SOUTH AMERICA,
Spanish colonial rulers
ignored local laws and
social customs and
imposed harsh new
rules, which treated
local people like slaves.

▷▷ ANTI-SLAVERY
campaigners in the
U.S. and Europe were
shocked by the way
slaves were treated
and punished.

△ SLAVES from Africa were sold at auctions when
they reached North America and the Caribbean.
Under the law, they became their new owners'
property, with few legal rights of their own.

▷ IN 1791, slaves in the French colony of Santo
Domingo (now Haiti) rebelled against colonial rule,
led by a former slave, Toussaint L'Ouverture.

◁ IN 1773, at the Boston Tea Party, American merchants in the British colonial town of Boston, Massachusetts, protested against unfair British trading laws by dumping British tea into Boston Harbor. In 1776, thirteen British colonies in America declared independence – defiantly breaking colonial law. Seven years of fighting followed. In 1787, the new nation – the United States of America – drafted the Constitution. It still forms the basis for all U.S. law.

In India, there were many different law codes, based on Hindu, Buddhist, Sikh, and Muslim religions. Local rulers also made their own laws; some were just, others were cruel and unfair. British and French colonial rulers often failed to understand Indian traditions, like suttee, and sometimes classified them as crimes. Religion and crime became confused, too, in the practice of Thuggee: robbery and ritual strangling by bandits devoted to the goddess Kali. The colonists' own practices, for example, the use of cow fat (holy to Hindus) and pig fat (unclean to Muslims) to grease army guns, also caused outrage and offense.

△ TRADITIONALLY, some Hindu women chose – or were persuaded – to follow the example of the goddess Sati. She committed suicide after her husband's death by leaping into the funeral pyre (cremation fire), to show her love and devotion. This custom was made illegal in 1829.

△ THE BUDDHA (Siddhartha Gautama, 563-483 BC) preached a 'universal law' of tolerance, compassion, and respect for all forms of life. He is revered today as the founder of one of the world's great religions.

In 1857, cultural misunderstandings and political discontent mingled together to produce the ultimate colonial "crime" – rebellion by Indian troops against British rule. Rebels were hunted down and executed, and their bodies were displayed in public.

▷ IN 1857, Indian troops in the British army rebelled against military orders that offended their religions.

△ SEPOY from Bengal. Almost 80 percent of the soldiers serving in the British East India Company's army were Indian.

△ MANY 1857 mutineers were executed.

▷ POLISHED STONE PILLAR, 7 feet (2.15m) high, built by King Ashoka at Sarnath, India, c. 250 B.C. It marks the holy site where Buddha first preached to his followers, telling them how they should live.

AFRICA AND THE PACIFIC

△ GOD MASK worn by Asante kings, of West Africa. Only kings could wear gold.

▷ FROM AROUND A.D. 800, northern Africa and eastern coastal districts were governed by Muslim rulers. Laws, learning, art, and architecture were strongly influenced by the teachings of Islam.

▷ CARVED FIGURES from ceremonial staffs (sticks) carried by chiefs in Bajokwe, West Africa.

AFTER AROUND A.D. 1000, northern and southern Africa were governed by different laws. North Africa, and some eastern coastal towns, were ruled by Muslim kings. Their laws were based on the Koran, and aimed to encourage fair trade, humane treatment of employees, and honest business deals. Failure to obey these laws was the most common crime. Along the east African coast, pirates raided merchant ships, and slavers kidnapped children to sell.

▽ THE ATA (king) of Igala, West Africa, at a council meeting, sketched by a European traveler, 1832-33. The Ata is wearing a royal mask.

◁ CARVED wooden throne made for a ruler in Cameroon, west Africa.

▷ THESE MASKS were worn with a flaming stick held between the jaws

▷ "KPONIUGO" mask from west Africa showing a magical creature who protected the community from soul stealers and sorcerers.

◁ DANCER from the Yoruba nation in Nigeria, taking part in a ceremony designed to pacify witches in the community by entertaining them. If the witches were displeased, they could bring lawlessness and disorder.

△ PORTRAIT sculpture of a king, from Nok in northern Nigeria, around 100 B.C.

▽ KING SHAMBA Bolongongo, who ruled in 17th-century Zaire. He was famous for his wise government.

◁ WOODEN BOWL to hold nuts used in ceremonies that foretold the future or aimed to "divine" the right thing to do.

▽ ABOVE RIGHT: the map shows the kingdom of Mansa Musa (died 1332), emperor of Mali. He ruled the richest nation in Africa according to Islamic law.

▷ BRONZE HEAD of a 17th-century king from Benin, West Africa.

◁ ABORIGINAL dance ceremony. Traditionally, dances like these strengthened the community.

Elsewhere in Africa, traditional beliefs shaped the law. Kings and their councils were the guardians of ancient ceremonies, designed to ensure good behavior by bonding communities together. Criminals were usually sold as slaves but they might be executed or killed as sacrifices. Many people believed in "magical" crime. Crops might fail or you might feel ill because of a curse sent by a criminal. East African *mganga* (sorcerers) said they could bewitch wild animals, then send them off to kill.

▽ ABORIGINAL MEN enrolled in the Australian police force. They aimed to maintain law and order in the wild frontier territory of Queensland, in the mid-19th century.

△ ELEVEN Australian farmhands, descended from English people transported to Australia, massacred 28 Aboriginals at Myall Creek in 1838. As punishment, seven of them were hanged.

▽ THE MAORI PEOPLE migrated to New Zealand from the Pacific Islands around A.D. 800. Led by chiefs, they settled the land and developed new laws.

▽ CARVED, tattooed wooden ancestral figure from New Zealand.

△ PACIFIC CHIEF'S ceremonial adze (wood-cutting tool). Right: The war god, Ku, from Hawaii.

In Australia and other Pacific lands, traditional laws were based on a community's struggle to survive in a harsh environment. Individuals had to work together or they might die. Guidance came from powerful spirits. Breaking spirit laws – which governed family life, hunting, fishing, and preparations for war – would lead to trouble.

▷ THE DJANGGAWUL BROTHER. According to myth, he and his sisters taught the Aboriginal people of Australia how to find water, grow crops, and organize their society.

△ ENGLISH JUDGE, 18th century. Some judges were wise and learned; others were brutal.

◁ A "CAUTIONARY TALE" of a criminal's career, popular with 18th-century artists:
1. Pickpocket.
2. Highwayman.
3. Arrested and tried in court.
4. In prison waiting for execution.

EUROPE 1700-1800

IN 18TH-CENTURY EUROPE, governments faced problems. Populations were growing, and crowded cities were thronged with noisy, excitable mobs of poorly paid workers, ready to riot against food shortages, increased taxes, or unpopular wars. People who could not find work – or who could not earn as much as they needed – turned to crime.

◁ CONDEMNED CRIMINALS were executed by hanging in public. Large crowds watched with mixed feelings of horror and fascination. Noble men and women were executed by beheading.

◁ ON BOARD SHIPS, sailors who disobeyed officers' orders were cruelly punished by flogging.

▷ WOMEN PIRATES Anne Bonney and Mary Read disguised themselves as men and went to sea.

◁ WRECKERS lured ships to the shore, then seized their cargoes when they foundered.

▽ CRIMES of war: soldiers looted and destroyed enemy towns, raped women, and killed men. They aimed to terrorize their opponents into submission.

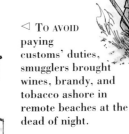

◁ TO AVOID paying customs' duties, smugglers brought wines, brandy, and tobacco ashore in remote beaches at the dead of night.

There were no police forces, so city tricksters, pickpockets, and burglars were hard to catch. In the country, in spite of mantraps and midnight patrols, poachers and smugglers often also managed to escape the law.

▷ IN 1715 and again in 1745, Jacobites in Scotland rebelled against the new Hanoverian kings in England. The rebels were defeated, and many were executed. After 1745, the Gaelic language of Scotland was banned and wearing the kilt became a serious offense.

▷ SUCCESSFUL CRIMINALS became popular heroes. Frenchman Louis Cartouche was the most famous gangster of his day.

△ CARTOUCHE was eventually caught, imprisoned, and executed in 1721.

◁ PISTOL-CARRYING highwaymen on fast horses waited to ambush wealthy travelers.

▷ FASHIONABLE noblemen challenged one another to a duel – usually "pistols at dawn" – if they felt they had been cheated or insulted.

▷ KING LOUIS XVI of France, his wife, Queen Marie Antoinette, and thousands of their royalist supporters were beheaded by the guillotine between 1792-94, during the French Revolution.

▽ IN 1831, farmworkers throughout England rioted for better pay and conditions.

Eighteenth-century governments were also challenged by new, revolutionary ideas. Philosophers debated "the rights of man." The French Revolution of 1789 was followed by the execution of the French royal family in 1793. As one mob leader said, now "monarchy was a crime." Soon, people in Europe and its colonies fought to "liberate" their countries from foreign control or to introduce new, democratic governments. Whether they were heroes or villains depended on your political views.

△ ON OCTOBER 14, 1789, at the start of the French Revolution, the starving working women of Paris marched to the royal palace at Versailles and brought back the heads of the royal bodyguards.

△ ONCE INSIDE JAIL, prisoners were often assaulted by guards.

EUROPE 1800-1914

DURING THE NINETEENTH CENTURY, for the first time, the study of crime and punishment was treated as a science. Philosophers like Jeremy Bentham (1748-1832) and Auguste Comte (1798-1857) put forward theories about what causes crime. Bentham hoped to reduce crime through "socially useful" laws, and to reform criminals by "scientific" punishments. These aimed at changing criminals' behavior, rather than locking them up.

Bentham's followers designed new prisons, where inmates could be observed and reeducated. But others disagreed with his ideas. Doctors believed that a "criminal tendency" was inborn; clergymen said that crime was the result of sin.

△ FROM THE 16th-19th centuries, night watchmen patrolled town streets after dark.

▽ VIOLENCE was common among prisoners; Newgate jail in the 19th century.

△ BODYSNATCHERS Burke and Hare murdered people to sell the bodies for medical research. Burke was convicted on Hare's evidence and executed in 1829. Hare died in poverty.

▷ IN NEW-STYLE 19th-century prisons, inmates were made to walk on a treadmill for miles every day.

△ REFORMERS like Elizabeth Fry (1780-1845) worked hard to improve prison conditions for women.

▽ THE FIRST POLICEMEN were appointed in London in 1829. They were called "peelers" after politician Sir Robert Peel.

Urchin

Pickpocket

In spite of Bentham's scientific studies and the humanitarian work of reformers like Elizabeth Fry, conditions in many nineteenth-century prisons, remained grim.

◁ FOOD was only available in exchange for hard labor in this yard at Bethnal Green Prison, London, 1868.

▽ HULKS were cold, damp, and crawling with rats and lice.

▽ CONVICTS waiting to be transported to Australia were kept in chains in hulks – old ships used as floating prisons.

△ BETWEEN 1787-1867, 160,000 convicts were transported to Australia in ships like this.

Crimes of all kinds seemed to be increasing throughout the nineteenth century, along with poverty, homelessness, and disease. The slum districts of Europe's big industrial cities were often criticized as breeding grounds of lawless violence. But the slums were full of low paid, badly treated workers. It is perhaps not surprising that riots, robberies, prostitution, and muggings were rife and political protesters found a ready audience there.

△ PRISON PUNISHMENTS were appalling. This flogging was reported in London newspapers in 1871.

▽ AFTER a series of murders in European capital cities in the 1880s, working women began to carry weapons.

▷ BIG-CITY STREETS throughout Europe were thronged with members of the criminal underclass.

Brawler

◁ IN GERMANY, anarchists were prosecuted for encouraging protests against government.

Gambler

▷ CIVIL DISOBEDIENCE: In 1911-12, militant suffragettes, demanding votes for women, smashed shop windows to protest government delays.

Prostitute

◁ GOVERNMENT CRIME: In 1819, radicals demanding reform of Parliament held a meeting at Peterloo, in Manchester, England. It was broken up by the army; 11 innocent protesters were killed.

After 1834 in England, poverty itself became a crime; people who could not find jobs were sent to a "workhouse" – deliberately built like a prison, with separate wings for men, women, and children, and fierce, stern wardens.

There were middle-class crimes, as well. Bankers and factory owners were fraudulent or careless, and many went bankrupt. Shopkeepers used false weights, gave short change, and adulterated foods with cheaper – often poisonous – substances.

UNITED STATES

THE UNITED STATES celebrated its first one hundred years as a nation in 1877. By then, it had become the richest, fastest growing, most confident society the world had ever seen. But there were problems. Rich businessmen, known as "robber barons," were accused of ruthless criminal tactics against rival companies. Campaigners exposed industrial scandals, such as child coal miners.

△ THE SPREAD of European technological "progress" across the U.S. often brought new crimes – like train robbery – with it.

▽ IN BIG CITIES, there was vandalism and attacks on property. These were sometimes motivated by racial hatred.

◁ IN CITIES, high-rises were good hiding places for criminals and conspirators, too.

▷ THE U.S. GOVERNMENT feared anarchists who encouraged disadvantaged groups in society to make violent protests.

▷ AL CAPONE (1899-1947), Mafia leader who organized contract killings, illegal alcohol trading, and financial fraud.

△ IN THE St. Valentine's Day Massacre, 1929, Al Capone's gunmen shot seven rival gangsters dead in Chicago.

◁ BONNIE PARKER and Clyde Barrow met in 1932. Together they committed many bank robberies and murders. They were shot dead by police in May 1934.

△ "TRIADS" – secret societies that were often involved in crime – operated among the Chinese community in many American cities.

▷ MEMBERS of the Mafia – a society originating in Sicily – made vast fortunes out of crime and killed anyone who dared to oppose them. They were also suspected of influencing local politics in several big American cities.

△ EXECUTION APPARATUS in the hospital ward at a correctional center. Convicted criminals are killed by a machine that injects three lethal drugs.

△ FOR MOST of the 20th century, the U.S. was the most prosperous nation in the world. Thus, big companies faced serious industrial crime – computer hacking and fraud.

Other events outraged the whole nation. In 1924, two rich white teenagers, Richard Loeb and Nathan Leopold, murdered a boy "for thrills." They were saved from the electric chair by the skill of America's most famous lawyer, Clarence Darrow, and sentenced to life imprisonment instead.

In 1920, the United States government introduced prohibition (banning the sale of alcohol), to reduce drunkenness. It did not work. The Mafia and other gangsters organized supplies of illegally produced liquor. Gangland warfare led to rapidly rising crime, and prohibition ended in 1933.

△ SINCE the 1940s, police, detectives, and "private eyes" have been popular heroes in American books and films, and on TV.

▷ THE KU KLUX KLAN is a white racist organization, founded in 1867. It once used bombings, lynchings, and whippings to attack African Americans. This Ku Klux Klan parade was held in Tulsa, Oklahoma, in 1933.

△ THE CHICAGO GANG known as Murder Inc, as photographed by the police in 1933.

CRIMES OF WAR

THERE HAVE ALWAYS BEEN CRIMES in wartime, sometimes as part of a deliberate policy of genocide (mass killing of enemies), sometimes by soldiers rampaging out of control. Civilians have usually suffered the most – over 300,000 were killed during the Thirty Years' War in Europe, between 1618-48. Armies have had court martials to punish soldiers who have broken military laws through carelessness, negligence, by refusing to obey orders or simply because of fear. The usual punishment for mutiny has been death. But often, war crimes against civilians or enemy prisoners have gone unpunished. Many civilizations have tried to limit the harm caused by war by laying down rules for "just" warfare. But without international willingness to uphold them, these rules have been difficult to enforce. After campaigns by the Swiss humanitarian reformer Henri Dunant, the first Geneva Convention was agreed to in 1864. It laid down rules for the fair treatment of wounded soldiers and prisoners of war. Dunant's work also led to the founding of the International Red Cross, a politically neutral organization that has saved thousands of lives in wartime by providing medical aid, emergency supplies and help for refugees.

◁ OVER 2 MILLION soldiers died in the trenches during World War I. Historians have called this a criminal waste of life.

△ NAZI WAR LEADERS, including Göring, Ribbentrop, and Hess, were convicted as criminals at the Nuremberg Trials, held 1945-46.

△ AFTER HITLER came to power in Germany in 1933, Jewish people were treated as "enemies of the state" and made to wear yellow stars. Between 1939-45, over 6 million Jews were imprisoned and murdered in Hitler's concentration camps.

▷ THE WORLD'S first atomic bomb was dropped on the Japanese port city of Hiroshima on August 6, 1945. Over 150,000 people were killed or injured; 75 percent of the city was destroyed.

◁ BETWEEN 1975-79, over 2.5 million Kampuchean people were massacred on the orders of ultra-communist dictator, Pol Pot, leader of a teenage guerrilla army, the Khmer Rouge.

△ THE "TROUBLES" in Northern Ireland lasted from 1968-1994. During that time, atrocities were committed by rival paramilitary groups from the Catholic and Protestant communities.

◁ TERRORIST GUNFIRE and bombs have destroyed lives and property in many parts of the world. Since 1948, the Middle East in particular has suffered from these crimes.

▷ THE CRIME OF GENOCIDE was used as a weapon during the Biafran War (1967-70) by the Nigerian government against the rebel Ibo people.

▷ MAO ZE-DONG (1893-1976), peasant leader of the Chinese Communists. He claimed: "Political power grows through the barrel of a gun." Toward the end of his life, his policies, as in the Cultural Revolution, became extreme and brutal.

▷ JOSEPH STALIN (1879-1953), general secretary of the Soviet Communist Party Central Committee from 1922 until his death. His collective farm policies led to millions of deaths from starvation; further millions of Soviet citizens were "purged" and sent to labor camps, exiled, or executed.

◁ NELSON MANDELA (born 1918) was sentenced to life imprisonment in 1964 for his opposition to the South African goverment's apartheid policy. He was freed in 1990, and elected the first black president of South Africa in 1994.

PRESENT AND FUTURE

MANY PEOPLE fear that society today is becoming more violent and criminal than ever before. In fact, this may not be true, but sinister new crimes are widespread – and experts cannot agree about what is causing them, or how they can be prevented in the future.

Large-scale drug distribution is organized by international gangs. There is a secret, but highly profitable, trade in weapons, including outlawed nerve gases and materials for making nuclear bombs. Citizens are distressed – but, sadly, also fascinated – to read about serial murders, sex crimes, or sickening violence. They also worry about crimes committed by teenagers against the most vulnerable groups in

△ GENETIC MANIPULATION techniques may make it possible to remove a "criminal" gene from a convicted offender or an unborn fetus. However, many scientists do not believe this will work.

▷ IF CRIME CONTINUED to increase, prison overcrowding might be solved by sending dangerous criminals to prisons built on colonies in space. There would be little danger of prisoners escaping, but what would living conditions in space be like?

△ RECONSTRUCTIONS of famous crimes and stories about the lives of violent criminals have become popular topics for films, television, and newspapers. In the 1990s, a few nations started to allow real police chases and actual trials to be televised live. Will this be the entertainment of the future?

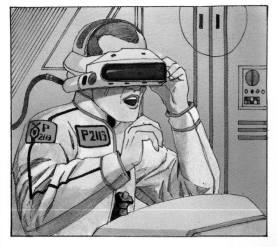

◁ INSTEAD of mid-20th-century-style schemes to try and reeducate and retrain violent criminals, computer-generated virtual reality might, in the future, be used to punish them. It would make criminals relive their crimes from their victims' point of view, so that they, too, would suffer fear and pain.

◁ PRISONS have been built on islands for centuries. The most famous was Alcatraz, a fortress built on a rocky island in deep water in San Francisco Bay. In the future, island prisons might be built with invisible force fields around them to make them escape proof.

society – old people and babies – who have traditionally been respected and cared for. Even "green" activists claim that present-day levels of pollution are a type of crime that will damage the world for centuries to come.

There is disagreement today about how to punish these – and other – crimes. Should punishment aim to show society's anger and to hurt the offender because they have hurt someone else? Should governments simply keep criminals locked away, where they can do no more harm? Or should prison and probation programs aim at reform? Planners looking toward the future are investigating all these possibilities, and more.

Roman Praetor (senior magistrate)

TIMELINE

B.C.
2351-2340 Reign of King Uru'inimgina, who issues the first-known Sumerian law code.
1792-1750 Reign of King Hammurabi of Babylon, famous as a lawmaker.

Sumerian legal contracts

c. 1370 Pharaoh Akhenaton attempts to introduce a new religion based on the worship of the sun disk. He builds a new city governed by new religious laws. But these "social experiments" collapse after his death.
c. 1200 Hebrew prophet Moses receives the Ten Commandments from God, on Mount Sinai. They form the basis of later Jewish law.
776 First Olympic Games, and the first special "Olympic Peace." It was designed to prevent crimes at the Games and among sportsmen and spectators traveling to them.

Ancient Egyptian court

c. 750 Greek poet Hesiod describes his ideal society governed by traditional country laws, watched over by the gods.
621 Athenian law-maker Draco introduces harsh new laws. Most crimes are punishable by death.
c. 600 Probable reign of Lycurgus, legendary lawmaker and ruler of the Greek city-state of Sparta.
594 Solon reforms many Athenian laws. Old punishments, for example, being enslaved for debt, are abolished.
c. 495-429 Pericles rules over the city of Athens at the height of its power. Athens is run as a democracy. Ordinary citizens take part in government, discuss new laws, and act as jurors in the courts.

Periander, tyrant of Corinth, c. 625-585 B.C.

403-222 Rise of "legalist" philosophy in China. Legalists aim to create a strong state and to discourage crime by a system of strict laws and very harsh punishments.
399 Death (by suicide) of Socrates, accused of teaching young people to criticize Athenian government and the law.
262 Emperor Asoka, ruler of the Maurya empire in India, becomes converted to Buddhism. Following this, he issues orders to all his subjects, encouraging them to live peaceful lives according to Buddhist religious laws.
221-206 Reign of first emperor of all China, Shih Huang Ti. He introduces stern new laws, tortures, and cruel punishments.
73-71 Revolt of Roman slaves led by Spartacus, a gladiator. Eventually, the slaves are defeated. Hundreds are crucified, and their bodies left hanging along the Appian Way – one of the main roads leading out of the city of Rome.
44 Murder of ambitious Roman dictator Julius Caesar.
31 Cleopatra, queen of Egypt, commits suicide after her country is conquered by the Romans.

A.D.
60 Queen Boudicca leads revolt against Roman conquerors of England.
54 Roman empress Agrippina poisons her husband, the emperor Claudius, so her son Nero can rule.
59 Nero arranges for Agrippina to be killed.
62 Nero orders his wife's murder and marries again.
65 Nero orders philosopher Seneca, his tutor, to commit suicide.
68 Nero is forced to commit suicide by his political opponents.
70 Mass suicide by Jews at Masada after Jewish state conquered by Rome.
200 Mishnah – collection of Jewish laws – compiled.
410 Visigoths (nomad tribes from the east) invade and destroy Rome.
506 Visigothic king Alaric II publishes new law code.
529 St. Benedict writes his Rule (laws) for Christian monasteries.
534 Roman emperor Justinian draws up new law code; this becomes the basis for later laws in much of southern Europe.
c. 570 Prophet Muhammad born in Arabia. Later revelations received from God become the basis of the Islamic faith and of Islamic law, known as shariyah.

Viking "Law of the Sword"

600 Pope Gregory writes a handbook giving rules for the behavior of Christian priests. Church law begins to develop.
604 New law code in Japan demands respect for the Buddha, Buddhist priests, and religious laws.
701 New Japanese law code regulates land ownership.
710 Roman emperor Justinian submits to the Pope's laws as head of the Roman Catholic Church.
716 Duke Lantfrid issues German law code.
782-808 King Charlemagne of France issues law codes.
793 First Viking pirate raids on coasts of England and Europe.
797 Byzantine empress Irene blinds her son, Constantine, so she can rule in his place.
801 Charlemagne makes prostitution a crime in France.
860 Famous forged document "The False Decretals" claims wide legal powers for the Pope.
890 King Alfred the Great of Wessex (England) extends the powers of royal courts.
900 New "shire" (county) courts in England provide reliable justice for ordinary people.
930 The first meeting of the Icelandic "Thing" – law court and parliament.
1119 University of Bologna founded. It becomes the greatest center of legal education in medieval Europe.
1170 Murder of Archbishop Thomas à Becket as part of quarrel over church and state laws.
1215 Trial by ordeal prohibited by Church.
1218 Newgate Prison in London built to house debtors.

Medieval Islamic punishment for stealing

1252 The Inquisition begins to use torture to investigate heresy in southern France.
1278 278 Jews hanged in London for clipping coins.
1314 Rich, powerful order of Knights Templars accused of heresy, and their leaders burned to death.
1369 The Bastille (large royal prison) built in Paris.
1465 King Edward IV of England makes laws against football hooliganism.
1530 New criminal code and police force introduced in Holy Roman Empire (Germany, Austria, Belgium, and Spain).
1553-1558 During the reign of Mary Tudor in England, over 300 Protestants are burned as heretics.
1597 First European convicts transported to the colonies.
1605 Guy Fawkes hung, drawn, and quartered as a traitor after the discovery of the Gunpowder Plot.
1626 Death penalty introduced for dueling in France.
1630 Pirate raids by buccaneers in the Caribbean.
1649 After losing Civil War in England, King Charles I tried and beheaded as a traitor.
1692 18 women executed after witch trials in Salem, Massachusetts.
1709 First Russian prisoners sent as exiles to Siberia.
1712 Last execution for witchcraft in England.
1739 English Highwayman Dick Turpin hanged.

1772 Judge William Murray rules that slaves become free if they set foot in England.
1774 Heinrich Pestalozzi founds first school for delinquent and disadvantaged children in Switzerland.
1789 Mutiny on the H.M.S. *Bounty*.
1793-94 Period of mass executions known as "the Terror" during the French Revolution. Around 40,000 "enemies of the revolution" die.
1806 First new high-security prison built in isolated site on Dartmoor, England.
1811 Civil disobedience campaign by Luddites – protesters who smash new industrial machines to try and save workers' jobs.
1818 To help stop city burglaries, American Jeremiah Chubb invents new security lock. In 1838, Charles Chubb invents burglarproof safe.

1823 The death penalty abolished for over 100 minor crimes – e.g. sheep-stealing – in England and Wales.
1840 French anarchist philosopher P.J. Proudhon claims "all property is theft."
1840 Last European criminal transported to Australia.
1843 American social reformer Dorothea Dix publishes report on shocking conditions in prisons and asylums.

19th-century public hanging

1865 First train holdup, North Bend, Ohio.
1881 Flogging abolished in British army and navy.
1888 Jack the Ripper murders 6 women in London.
1902 Britain sets up concentration camps for Boer (Dutch settler) enemy prisoners during Boer War in South Africa.

1904 In New York, a policeman arrests a woman for smoking in public.
1910 Englishman Dr. H.H. Crippen executed after poisoning three wives.
1913 First woman magistrate (local judge) in England.
1917 Suffragettes campaign for votes for women in England. They are imprisoned, go on hunger strike, and are force-fed.
1921 Sweden becomes the first country to abolish capital punishment.
1924 German serial killer Fritz Haarmann condemned to death for 26 murders.
1925 First international conference on drugs and crime.
1929 St. Valentine's Day gangland massacre, Chicago.
1932 Kidnap and murder of baby of famous American air ace Charles Lindbergh.
1934 Robbers and mass killers Bonnie Parker (born 1910) and Clyde Barrow (born 1909) shot dead by Louisiana police.
1944 The "Great Escape": 50 British officers killed while breaking out of a German prisoner-of-war camp.
1945 "Black Markets" selling illegal supplies of rationed goods throughout Europe.
1945-46 Nuremberg War Trials. Many Nazi leaders condemned. Concentration camp commanders also tried, including Ilse Koch ("the beast of Buchenwald").

Angry mob, 19th century

1950s "Cold War" between U.S.S.R. and U.S.A. and their allies. Many spy trials. In U.S.A., alleged communists are accused of disloyalty; many lose their jobs.
1963 American president John F. Kennedy assassinated. Some believe this was the work of government intelligence agencies, who disliked Kennedy's policies.

20th-century computer crime

1964 The "Great Train Robbery" in England. The 12 robbers who seized valuable mail from a train were sentenced to a total of 307 years in prison.
1966 "Moors Murders" – Britons James Brady and Myra Hindley torture and kill young children, then bury them on the moors.
1970s Many terrorist attacks – bombings, hijackings, etc. – by political activists.
1980s Increase in football hooliganism and street crimes. Growing concern over drug-related crime, armed teenage gangs, and use of guns in crime worldwide.
1990s Widespread public belief – after murder of U.K. toddler James Bulger by two older children – that violent films, videos, and TV programs may encourage violent crime among young people, but experts disagree.

GLOSSARY

Anarchists People who are opposed to governments and state powers, including laws and courts.

Apartheid Legal system in South Africa (ended 1990s) discriminating on grounds of race and color, giving unfair advantages to white people.

Collective farm A large area farmed by groups of peasants for the good of the whole community, rather than for individual profit.

Colonial A system of government where one country is ruled by another, stronger one.

Concentration camp A prison where political opponents are kept and often treated very badly or even murdered.

Confiscated Taken away.

Conspirators Plotters.

Constitution The rules by which a country is run. Sometimes they are a set of laws; sometimes they are a collection of unwritten traditions.

Contract killing A murder carried out by professional killers on someone else's orders.

Crusades Wars between Christian and Muslim soldiers fought between 1095-1291 over the right to control sacred sites in the Holy Land (present-day Israel and nearby lands).

Cultural Revolution (1966-76) A mass movement among Chinese Communists, designed by Chinese leader Mao Zhedong, to destroy all traditional powers in Chinese society.

Democratic Ruled by a majority vote of ordinary people.

Dictator A single ruler who takes complete control of a nation.

Dissident Someone who disagrees with the ruler or political system of their state.

Exiled Forced to live away from your homeland.

Feudal A way of organizing society in which land is granted by lords to peasants in return for military service or work.

Flogging Beating.

Genocide Systematic killing of one race of people by another.

Guerrilla Soldier who fights by surprise raids instead of pitched battles.

Guild An association of craft workers that regulated the quality of finished goods, provided training, and negotiated the terms of workers' pay and conditions.

Hanoverian A dynasty of British kings, originally from Germany, who ruled from 1714 to 1901.

Heresy Religious opinions that challenge accepted beliefs. In the Middle Ages in Europe, heresy was treated as a crime.

Heretics People who hold religious opinions that challenge accepted beliefs.

Hoodlums Young, lawless men in the Wild West.

Inquisitions Trials held by church lawyers in cases of suspected heresy.

Islam One of the major world faiths, taught by the prophet Muhammad (c. 570-632). Islam means "submission to God." People who follow the faith of Islam are known as Muslims.

Jacobites A political group, based in Scotland, that opposed the Hanoverian dynasty (see above) and supported rival claimants to the throne.

Koran The holy book of Islam. It contains revelations sent to the prophet Muhammad by God.

Labor camp Prison where prisoners are forced to work.

Law Code Collection of laws.

Lynching Execution of a suspected criminal by a mob, without a proper trial.

Mogul The ruling Muslim dynasty of India, 1526–1857.

Mongols Nomadic people who lived in Central Asia.

Nazi The German National Socialist party, responsible for many crimes and atrocities during World War II.

Ostracize In ancient Greece, to exile for ten years.

Pillory A wooden frame inside which petty criminals were locked for public humiliation.

Purged (political) Dismissed from office and exiled or executed.

Pyre Bonfire where dead bodies are cremated (burned).

Recant Give up former beliefs.

Rhyton Drinking cup made out of a ram's horn.

Samurai Japanese landowner who followed a strict warrior lifestyle.

Suttee Ritual suicide by widows in India.

Senate In Rome, a group of retired state officials who debated government policies and made new laws.

Shariyah Islamic law, covering all areas of life, based on the Koran.

Shogun Top Japanese general.

Slander Harmful, untrue words.

Spirit bundle Collection of objects (stones, feathers, etc.) representing magical spirit powers.

Sorcerer Magician.

Thing Viking law-making assembly.

Torah Jewish religious law.

Tyrant Single, strong ruler, who ignores the wishes of the people he rules.

Virtual reality Computer-based experience that aims to recreate our experience of the real world.

Zen Japanese Buddhist religious movement, which began in the thirteenth century.

INDEX